Piano/Vocal

Simon and Garfunkel
Bridge Over Troubled Water

Baby Driver, 30

Bridge Over Troubled Water, 2

Bye Bye, Love, 44

Cecilia, 10

El Condor Pasa, 7

Keep The Customer Satisfied, 14

So Long, Frank Lloyd Wright, 17

Song For The Asking, 46

The Boxer, 22

The Only Living Boy In New York, 33

Why Don't You Write Me?, 39

Distributed by
Music Sales Limited,
8/9 Frith Street,
London W1V 5TZ,
England.

Bridge Over Troubled Water

Words and Music by
PAUL SIMON

© 1969, 1970 PAUL SIMON
International Copyright Secured
All Rights Reserved

Eb Ab Eb Bb Cm Bb
I'm on your side. Oh,
I'll take your part. Oh,
mp
Bb9 Eb Eb (D bass) In tempo Eb7 Eb9 Ab F
when times get rough
when dark - ness comes
And friends just can't be found,
And pain is all a - round,
f
Bb Eb7 Eb9 Ab F#dim (A bass) Eb (Bb bass) C7sus C7
Like a Bridge O - ver Trou-bled Wa-ter
mp
Ab G7 Cm Eb7 Eb9 Ab F#dim (A bass) 1. Eb (Bb bass) C7sus C7
I will lay me down. Like a Bridge O - ver Trou-bled Wa-ter
mf
mp

Ab
Bb9 (sus)
Bb7
Eb
Ab
I will lay me down.
mf
f
Eb
Ab
Eb
Ab
Rubato
When you're
mf
mp
mf
mp
p
2
Eb (Bb bass)
Cm
Ab
Cm (G bass)
G
Cm
F7
Trou-bled Wa-ter I will lay me down.
mf
f
Eb
Ab
Cm
Ab
Abm
Eb

Ab
Eb
Ab
Eb
Ab
Sail on
Eb
Ab
Db
Ab
sil - ver girl,
Sail on by.
Your time has
Eb
Ab
Eb
Ab
Eb
Ab
come to shine.
All your dreams are on their way.
Eb
Bb
Cm
Bb
Eb
Eb
(D bass)
See how they shine.
Oh,
if you need a friend
mp

In tempo
Eb7
Eb9
Ab
F
Bb
Eb7
Eb9
Ab
F#dim
(A bass)
I'm sail - ing right be - hind. Like a Bridge O - ver
f
Eb
(Bb bass)
Cm
Ab
Cm
G
Cm
Eb7
Eb9
Ab
Ab maj7
F7
(A bass)
Trou-bled Wa-ter I will ease your mind. Like a Bridge O - ver
mf
f
ff
Eb
(Bb bass)
Cm
Ab
G7
Cm
F9
Fmaj9
Trou - bled Wa-ter I will ease your mind.
Eb
(Bb bass)
Ab
Abm
Eb
rall.
fff

El Condor Pasa

Musical Arrangement by
J. MILCHBERG and D. ROBLES

English Lyric by
PAUL SIMON

© 1933, 1963, 1970 EDWARD B. MARKS MUSIC CORP. and JORGE MILCHBERG
English Lyric © 1970 CHARING CROSS MUSIC, INC.
International Copyright Secured All Rights Reserved

G
C
G
swan that's here and gone. A man gets tied up to the ground, He gives the world its sad-dest
Em
sound, its sad-dest sound. I'd rath-er be a for-est than a
G
Em
street. Yes I would. If I could, I sure-ly would. I'd rath-er feel the earth be-neath my
G
Em
C
3
feet.. Yes I would. If I on-ly could, I sure-ly would.
3
G
C

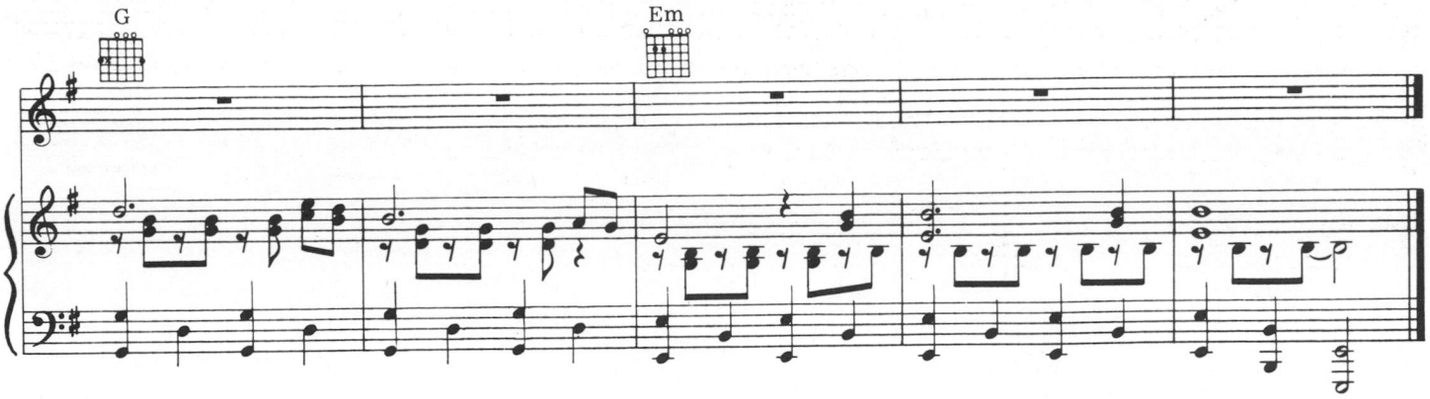
G
Em

Cecilia

Words and Music by
PAUL SIMON

© 1969, 1970 PAUL SIMON
International Copyright Secured
All Rights Reserved

B♭
F
1. C
2. C
beg-ging you please to come home.
Ho - ho - home.
F
B♭
Mak - ing love in the af - ter - noon with Ce - ci -
F
B♭
F
C
F
(mak - ing love)
- lia, Up in my bed - room,
I got up to wash
B♭
F
C
F
my face When I come back to bed, some-one's tak - en my place.

F Bb F Bb F
Cel - ia, You're break-ing my heart, You're shak-ing my con - fi-dence dai -
mf
C Bb F Bb F
- ly. Oh, Ce - cil - ia, I'm down on my knees, I'm
Bb F C F
beg-ging you please to come home. Come on home. Poh poh
mp
mf
F Bb C
Fsus
poh poh poh poh poh poh poh poh poh poh poh. Ju - bi -

Bb F Bb F Bb F
la - tion, She loves me a - gain, I fall on the floor and I laugh-
f mf
1. C 2. C Bb F
- ing. Ju - bi - - ing. Oh oh oh oh oh oh
1. 2. f
Bb F Bb F 1. C
oh oh oh oh oh oh oh oh oh oh oh oh oh. Oh oh
f
2. C
oh. Come on home.
mf rall.

Keep The Customer Satisfied

Words and Music by
PAUL SIMON

© 1970 PAUL SIMON
International Copyright Secured
All Rights Reserved

Eb
Bb
Eb
slan - dered, Li - beled, I hear words I nev - er heard In the Bi -
Ab
Eb
Cm
Eb
- ble. And I'm one step a-head of the shoe shine, Two steps a-way from the
Cm
Ab
Eb
Eb7
Ab
1. Eb
coun-ty line, Just trying to keep my cus-tom-ers sat - is - fied, Sat - is - fied.
2. Eb
fied. Woh Woh
f
Ab
(Ab bass)
Eb
Woh Woh

Eb Ab Eb
But it's the same old sto - ry
Ab Eb Bb Eb
Ev - 'ry-where I go, I get slan-dered, Li - beled, I hear words
Ab Eb
I nev - er heard In the Bi - ble. And I'm so
Cm Eb Cm Bb
tired, I'm oh so tired, But I'm
Eb Eb7 Ab Eb Ab7
trying to keep my cus-tom-ers sat - is - fied, Sat - is - fied.

So Long, Frank Lloyd Wright

Words and Music by
PAUL SIMON

© 1969, 1970 PAUL SIMON
International Copyright Secured
All Rights Reserved

F
Gm
E♭maj7
So soon
So soon.
Em7-5
D
I'll re - mem - ber
mf
D7
B♭7
C
F6noC
Frank Lloyd Wright.
mf
mp
A7
Dm
Dm7
F7
B♭maj7
All of the nights we'd har - mo - nize till dawn.

Bb
F
I nev - er laughed so long So long
Gm
Gb
Gbmaj7
F
So long.
F7
Gm7
Fmaj7
Ar - chi-tects may come and Ar - chi - tects may go and nev -
Eb9
F
Gm7
Fm7
- er change your point of view.
When I
mf
dim. poco - - -

E♭7
E♭7-5
D7-5
Gmaj7
G7
C♯dim
G7
run dry I stop a - while and think of you.
- a - - poco
Gm7
Fmaj7
Ar - chi - tects may come and Ar - chi - tects may go and nev -
mp
E♭9
F
Dmaj7
- er change your point of view.
So
D7
B♭7
C
F6noC
Long,
Frank Lloyd Wright,
mp
mf
mp

A7
Dm
Dm7
F7
B♭maj7
All of the nights we'd har - mo - nize till dawn.
f
B♭
F
I nev - er laughed so long
So long
mf
mp
Keep repeating and fade out
G
G♭
F
G♭add A
So long
So long
dim. poco a poco
G
G♭
G♭maj7
F
G♭add A
So long.
So long

The Boxer

Words and Music by
PAUL SIMON

© 1969 PAUL SIMON
International Copyright Secured
All Rights Reserved

Am
G
F
All lies and jest, still a man hears what he wants to hear, And
C
G
dis - re - gards the rest.
C
When I left my home and my fam - i - ly, I was

Am
G
no more than a boy in the com - pa - ny of stran - gers in the
Dm7
C
qui - et of a rail - way sta - tion run - ning scared,
Am
C
F
Lay - ing low, seek - ing out the poor - er quar - ters where the
G
F
Em
Dm
rag - ged peo - ple go, Look-ing for the plac - es on - ly they would

C
Am
know.
Lie - la - lie,
Lie - la -
G
Am
G
lie la lie - la - lie lie - la - lie
Lie - la -
F
G
C
lie la la la la Lie - la la la la lie.
Ask - ing on - ly work - man's wag - es I come

Am
G
look-ing for a job, but I get no of - fers, Just a

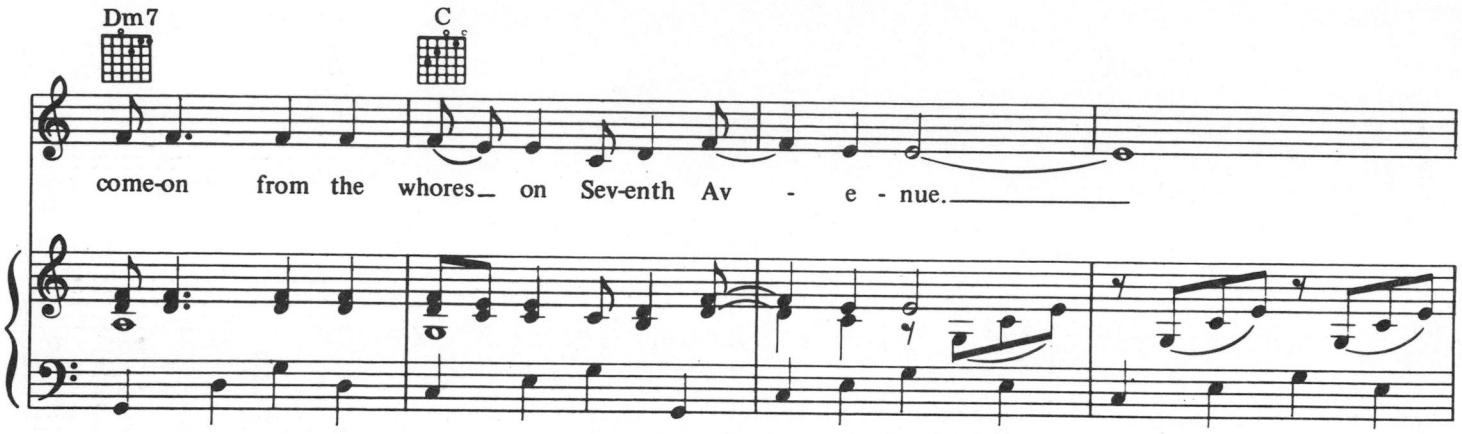
Dm7
C
come-on from the whores on Sev-enth Av - e - nue.

Am
Dm7
G
F
I do de - clare, there were times when I was so lone-some I

C
G
took some com-fort there. Ooo - la - la la - la la la.

C
C
Then I'm lay - ing out my
G7
C
Am
G
win - ter clothes and wish - ing I was gone, go - ing home
Dm7
G7
G
C
Where the New York Cit - y win - ters are - n't bleed - ing me,
Em
Am
Lead - ing me,

G
C
go - ing home.
C
In the clear - ing stands a box - er, and a fight - er by his
Am
G
G7
trade, And he car - ries the re - mind - ers of ev - 'ry glove that
C
Dm7
G7
C
laid him down Or cut him till he cried out in his an - ger and his shame,

Am G F C
"I am leav - ing, I am leav - ing." But the fight - er still re-mains.
G C G F C
Lie - la
Fade
Am G Am
lie, Lie - la - lie la lie -la - lie Lie - la - lie
G F C
Lie - la lie la la la la lie - la la la la lie. Lie - la

Baby Driver

Words and Music by
PAUL SIMON

© 1969 PAUL SIMON
International Copyright Secured
All Rights Reserved

G
gray morn With mu - sic com - in' in my ears
ried a gun But I nev - er got the chance to serve
a - lone Oh, come in - to my room and play
D
In my ears. They call
I did not serve. They call
Yes, we can play. I'm not talk -
G
me Ba - by Driv - er, And once u - pon a pair of wheels
me Ba - by Driv - er, And once u - pon a pair of wheels
in' a - bout your pig - tails, But talk - in' 'bout your sex ap - peal
D
D
Db
Am
B7
3
Hit the road and I'm gone ah What's my num - ber, I
Hit the road and I'm gone ah What's my num - ber, I
Hit the road and I'm gone ah What's my num - ber, I

Em
Em7
won - der how your en - gine feels. Ba Ba Ba Ba
won - der how your en - gine feels. Ba Ba Ba Ba
won - der how your en - gine feels. Ba Ba Ba Ba
D
Db
Am
B7
Scoot down the road, What's my num - ber, I
Scoot down the road, What's my num - ber, I
Scoot down the road, What's my num - ber, I
Em7
D
won - der how your en - gine feels.
won - der how your en - gine feels.
won - der how your en - gine feels.
1, 2.
3.
2. My
3. My
Repeat and fade

The Only Living Boy In New York

Words and Music by
PAUL SIMON

© 1969, 1970 PAUL SIMON
International Copyright Secured
All Rights Reserved

C
F
Am7
Dm7
F
Fly down to Mex - i - co.
G
F
Da - n - da - da - n - da - da - n - da - da and here I am, The
mf
mp
C
F
C
On - ly Liv-ing Boy In New York.
r.h.
F
C
Dm7
C
F
I get the news I need from the weath-er re - port.
r.h.

C
I can gath - er all the news I need from the weath - er re - port.
F
C
Hey, I've got noth-ing to
r.h.
mf
3
F
C
Dm
F6
G
do to - day but smile. Da - n - da - da - n - do - da - n - do - n
F
C
here I am, The On - ly Liv - ing Boy In New
mp

F
Am
York.
r.h.
mf
Dm
G7
C
Half of the time we're gone but we don't know where, And we don't know
f
dim. poco a poco
C
where. Tom, get your plane right on
mp
3
F
C
time. I know that you've been ea - ger to fly
r.h.

F
C
now.
Hey
let your hon - es - ty
mf
F
C
Dm
F
G
shine, shine, shine now,
Do - da - n - do - da - n - do -
Fmaj7
F6
F
da - n - do like it shines on me.
The
mp
C
F
On - ly Liv - ing Boy In New York.
The

C F C

On - ly Liv-ing Boy In New York.

p r.h. rall. pp

Why Don't You Write Me?

Words and Music by
PAUL SIMON

© 1969, 1970 PAUL SIMON
International Copyright Secured
All Rights Reserved

Cm
Gm
- ing so hard to be near you.
Eb
Ab
Eb
(Falsetto:) La la la.
(Basso) Why don't you write?
(Sing:)
Some-thing is wrong
F7
and I know I got to be there.
(yeah)
Bb7
May - be I'm lost, but I can't make the cost of the air -

Cm
Gm
Eb
Ab
fare.
(oo)
Tell me why
Why
mf
Bb
Tell me why
Why
Why
Why
Eb
Why Don't You Write Me? A let - ter would bright - en my lone-
mp
F7
- li - est eve - ning.
Bb7
Mail it to - day if it's on -

Cm
Gm
- ly to say that you're leav - ing me. (Oo)
Eb
Ab
Eb
Eb7
(Falsetto:) La la la.
p
mp
Ab7
(Sing:) Mon-day morn-ing, sit-ting in the sun Hop - ing and wish-ing for the mail to come.
mf
Eb
Eb7
Ab7
Tues-day, nev-er got a word, mmm. Wednes-day, Thurs-day, ain't no sign, Drank
mp
mf

E♭
a half a bot - tle of i - o - dine. Fri - day, woe is me, I'm
E♭7
A♭
gliss.
gon - na hang my bod - y from the high - est tree. (Falsetto:) Why Don't You Write
mf
E♭
A♭
Me?
(Sing:) Why Don't You Write Me?
dim. poco a poco
A♭7
E♭
Why Don't You Write Me?
Why Don't You Write

Bye Bye, Love

By FELICE BRYANT and
BOUDLEAUX BRYANT

© Copyright 1957 by ACUFF-ROSE PUBLICATIONS INC.
Reprinted by permission of ACUFF-ROSE MUSIC LTD., 15 St. George Street, London W1
International Copyright Secured All Rights Reserved

CHORUS
Bb F Bb F Bb
BYE BYE, LOVE: Bye Bye, hap - pi- ness; Hel- lo
F C7 F Bb F
LONE-li- ness I think I'm gon - na cry; BYE BYE, LOVE;
Bb F Bb F C
Bye bye, sweet ca- ress; Hel - lo emp- ti- ness; I feel like I could die;
F C7 1 F 2 F
Bye bye, my love, bye bye. bye.

Song For The Asking

Words and Music by
PAUL SIMON

© 1970 PAUL SIMON
International Copyright Secured
All Rights Reserved

Eb Bb Eb F7 Bb
wait - ing all my life.
Gm Dm D Bdim Cm F7
Think-ing it o-ver, I've been sad, Think-ing it o-ver, I'd be more than glad To
Bb Bb7 G Eb Gm Cm7
change my ways for the ask - ing, Ask me and I will
D D7 Eb Bb Eb Bb F7 Bb
play All the love that I hold in-side.

Printed by JB Offset Printers
(Marks Tey) Ltd
Station Approach, North Lane
Marks Tey, Colchester, Essex

11/89 9650